PIANO • VOCAL • GUITAR

ROCK REVIVAL

40 TOP HITS FROM THE EARLY ROCK ERA

HAL LEONARD
PUBLISHING
CORPORATION

Home Office: National Sales Office:
960 East Mark Street 7777 West Bluemound Road
Winona, MN 55987   Milwaukee, WI 53213

ISBN 0-88188-943-1

7.95

PIANO · VOCAL · GUITAR

ROCK REVIVAL

40 TOP HITS FROM THE EARLY ROCK ERA

0881889431 03 B6

CONTENTS

Rnk 163
Blue shed

ALL SHOOK UP

Words and Music by OTIS BLACKWELL
and ELVIS PRESLEY

Medium Shuffle Rhythm

A - well - a, bless my soul,__ What's wrong with me?__ I'm itch-ing like a man__ on a

fuz-zy tree__ My friends say I'm act-in' queer as a bug__ I'm in love I'm

all shook up!__ Mm__ mm oh, oh, yeah,__ yeah!_____ My

hands are sha-ky and my knees are weak.___ I can't seem to stand___ on my

own two feet,___ Who do you thank when you have such luck?___ I'm in

Eb7   **F7**

love!   I'm all shook up!___ Mm___ mm   oh,   oh,   yeah,___

Bb **Eb7** **Bb**   **Eb7**

yeah!_____

Please don't ask what's on my mind,___ I'm a
Tongue gets tied when I try to speak,___ My

lit - tle mixed up but I'm feel - in' fine ___ When I'm near that girl that
in - sides shake like a leaf on a tree, There's on - ly one cure for this

I love best, My That's to heart beats so it scares me to death! She
soul of mine, have the girl that I love ___ so ___ fine! ___

touched my hand, What a chill I got, ___ Her kiss - es are like ___ a vol -

ca - no that's hot! ___ I'm proud to say she's my but - ter - cup, ___ I'm in

AT THE HOP

Words and Music by ARTHUR SINGER,
JOHN MEDORA and DAVID WHITE

BLUE SUEDE SHOES

Words and Music by CARL LEE PERKINS

Bright Tempo (not too fast)

Chorus

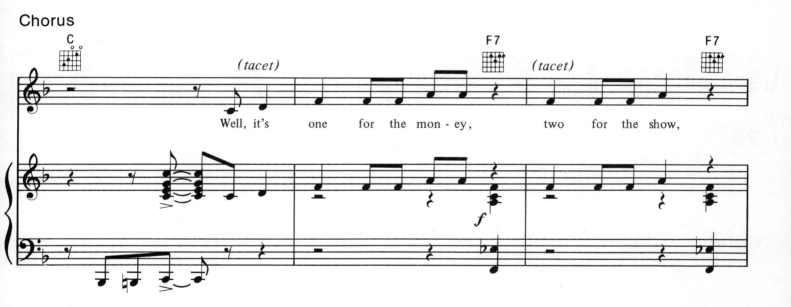

Well, it's one for the mon-ey, two for the show,

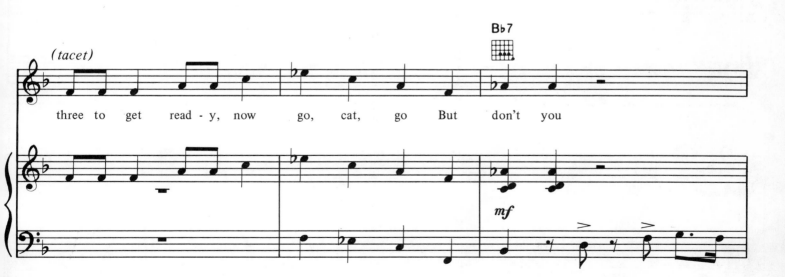

three to get read-y, now go, cat, go But don't you

BABY, I'M YOURS

Moderately, with a beat

Words and Music by
VAN McCOY

CHANTILLY LACE

Moderate Boogie Woogie

Words and Music by J.P. RICHARDSON

Oh, Baby, you know what I like!

C7

Chan - til - ly lace ____ and a pret - ty face ____

F

____ and a pon - y tail ____ hang - in' down, ____ Wig - gle in her

C7

walk and a gig - gle in her talk,

F

Makes the world go 'round ___

Ain't noth-in' in this world like a big eyed girl __ to make me act so fun-ny, make me spend my mon-ey, make me feel real loose like a long-necked goose, like a girl. *Spoken: Oh, Baby,* *that's-a what I like.*

girl. *Spoken: Oh, Baby,* *that's - a what I like.*

BLUEBERRY HILL

Words and Music by
AL LEWIS, LARRY STOCK and VINCENT ROSE

CHAPEL OF LOVE

Words and Music by
PHIL SPECTOR, ELLIE GREENWICH
and JEFF BARRY

COME GO WITH ME

Words and Music by C.E. QUICK

DON'T BE CRUEL
(To A Heart That's True)

Words and Music by OTIS BLACKWELL
and ELVIS PRESLEY

DAWN (GO AWAY)

Words and Music by BOB GAUDIO
and SANDY LINZER

Pret-ty as a mid-sum-mer's morn, They call her Dawn.

Dawn, _____ go a - way, I'm no good for you, _____
Dawn, _____ go a - way back where you be - long, _____

1

Dm · G7 · C

Al - tho' I know_____ I want you to stay.

2

Fm · G7

Ba - by, don't cry,_____ it's bet - ter this

Eb · F · G · Eb · F · G7 · **D.S. al Coda**

way._____ Ah_____ (Oh_____)

CODA · C6 · F · **Repeat and Fade**

Dawn,_____ go a - way, I'm no good for you._____ Oh,___

DUKE OF EARL

Moderately with a rock beat

Words and Music by EARL EDWARDS
EUGENE DIXON and BERNICE WILLIAMS

As ____ I _____ walk through this world,
When _____ I hold ___ you,

No - thing can stop the
You ___ will be the the

Duke of Earl, ___ And you _____ are my girl, ____ And
Duch - ess of Earl, When I walk _____ through my Duke - dom, The

no one can hurt you, Yes I'm ____
par - a - dise we will share, I'm _____

EARTH ANGEL

Words and Music by
DOOTSIE WILLIAM

Slowly with a beat

Earth an - gel, earth an - gel, Will you be mine,— My dar - ling, dear,—

Love you all the time.— I'm just a fool,— A fool in love with

you.— Earth an - gel, earth an - gel,

GREAT BALLS OF FIRE

Words and Music by OTIS BLACKWELL
and JACK HAMMER

THE GREEN DOOR

Words and Music by BOB DAVI
and MARVIN MOOR

HE'S A REBEL

Moderately, with a beat

Words and Music by
GENE PITNEY

See the way he walks down the street,
When he holds my hand I'm so proud,

watch the way he shuf-fles his feet,
'Cause he's not just one of the crowd,

Oh, how he holds his head high when
My ba-by's al-ways the one to

he goes walk-in' by_____ He's my guy!_____

HEARTBREAK HOTEL

By MAE BOREN AXTON,
TOMMY DURDEN and ELVIS PRESLEY

IT'S MY PARTY

Words and Music by HERB WIENER,
WALLY GOLD and JOHN GLUCK, JR.

Moderately bright

No-bod-y knows____ where my John-ny has gone,____ But
Play all my rec — ords, keep danc-ing all night,____ But
Ju-dy and John — ny just walked thru the door,____ But

Ju - dy left____ the same time.
leave me a-lone____ for a — while,
Like a queen____ with her king,

Why was he
'Til John-ny's
Oh, what a

LOLLIPOP

With a beat

Words and Music by BEVERLY ROS
and JULIUS DIXO

Lol-li-pop, lol-li-pop, Oh,_____ lol-li, lol-li, lol-li, lol-li-pop, lol-li-pop, Oh,__

_____ lol-li, lol-li, lol-li, lol-li-pop, lol-li-pop, Oh,_____ lol-li, lol-li, lol-li,

lol-li-pop.

Call my ba-by lol-li-pop,
Cra-zy way she thrills-a me,

LOUIE, LOUIE

Medium Rock beat

Words and Music by RICHARD BERRY

Uh Lou - ie, Lou - ie,___ oh, no,___ say - in'

we got - ta go. Yeah, yeah, yeah, yeah, yeah. Said uh Lou - ie, Lou - ie,___

oh, ba - by,___ said___ we got - ta go.

A
Three
Me

LONG TALL SALLY

Words and Music by ENOTRIS JOHNSON,
RICHARD PENNIMAN and ROBERT BLACKWELL

Bright rock tempo

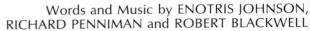

have some fun to-night,___ Gon-na have some fun to-night

___ woo!___ We're gon-na have some fun to-night___

Ev-'ry-thing will be all right.___ We're gon-na have some fun, gon-na

have some fun to-night!_____

RUNAWAY

Bogre
164

Moderately bright

Words and Music by DEL SHANNON
and MAX CROOK

As I walk a - long___ I won - der what went wrong___ with

our love, a love that was___ so strong.

And as I still walk on___ I think of the things we've done___ to -

MY BOYFRIEND'S BACK

Words and Music by ROBERT (BOB) FELDMAN,
GERALD (JERRY) GOLDSTEIN and RICHARD GOTTEHRER

Moderately

RAG DOLL

Words and Music by BOB CREWE
and BOB GAUDIO

SAVE THE LAST DANCE FOR ME

Words and Music by DOC POMUS
and MORT SHUMAN

Eb

Bb7

home and in whose arms you're gon - na be. ___ So dar - lin', ___ save the

1 Eb

2 Eb

last dance for me. Oh, I me.

Bb7

Guitar Tacet

Ba - by, don't you know I love you so? ___ Can't you feel it when we

Eb

Guitar Tacet

Bb7

touch? I will nev - er, nev - er let you go. ___ I love you, oh, so

SIXTEEN CANDLES

Words and Music by LUTHER DIX
and ALLYSON R. KH

SEA OF LOVE

Words and Music by GEORGE KHOU
and PHILIP BAST

2
G
D
C
Come with me
D
C
B7
D
D.C. al Coda
(verse 1)
D7
to the sea of love.
CODA
G
Guitar Tacet
Eb
Db
Come with me
Eb
Db
C7
to the sea of

SPLISH SPLASH

Moderately, with a beat

Words and Music by BOBBY DARIN
and JEAN MURRAY

how was I to know there was a par - ty go - ing on?
went and put my danc - ing shoes___

on I was a - splish - in' and a - splash - in', I was a -

roll - in' and a - stroll - in', I was a - mov - in' and a - groov - in',

I was a - reel - in' with the feel - in' I was a -

Repeat and Fade

STAND BY ME

Words and Music by BEN E. KING,
JERRY LEIBER and MIKE STOLLER

SUGAR SHACK

Words and Music by KEITH McCORMACK
and FAYE VOSS

1. There's a cra-zy lit-tle house _____ be-yond the tracks, _____
2. cute _____ lit-tle girl-y, she's a-work-ing there, _____
3. Sug-ar Shack _____ queen _____ is a-mar-ried to me, _____

And ev-'ry-bod-y calls it the
Black le-o-tards and her
We just sit a-round and dream of those

THE STROLL

With a moderately strong rock beat

Words and Music by CLYDE O
and NANCY L

Come, let's stroll, _____ stroll a - cross the floor __

Come, let's stroll, _____ stroll a - cross the floor _

Now turn a - round, ba - by,

stroll_____ There's my love_____ stroll-ing in the door__

_____ There's my love_____ stroll-ing in the door

Ba - by, let's go stroll - ing by the can - dy

store.

store._____

SUMMERTIME BLUES

Words and Music by EDDIE COCHRAN
and JERRY CAPEHART

A TEENAGER IN LOVE

Words and Music by DOC POMU
and MORT SHUMAN

Moderately slow

Each time we have a quar-rel it al-most breaks my heart,
One day I feel so hap-py; next day I feel so sad.

'Cause I am so a-fraid that we will have to part.
I guess I'll learn to take the good with the bad.

Each night I ask the stars up a-bove:

Why must I be a teen - ag - er in love?

I cried a tear for no - bod - y but you.

I'll be a lone - ly one if you should say we're through.

If you want to make me cry, that won't be so hard to do.

TELL LAURA I LOVE HER

Words and Music by JEFF BARRY
and BEN RALEIGH

that can - not wait.''

He drove his car to the rac - ing grounds,— He was the young-est

driv - er there;— The crowd roared as they start - ed the race, 'Round the

track they drove— at a dead - ly pace!— No one knows what

hap-pened that day,— How his car o-ver-turned in flames,— But

as they pulled him from the twist-ed wreck,— With his dy - ing breath,— they

heard him say:— "Tell Lau - ra I love her!

Tell Lau - ra I need her! Tell Lau - ra not to cry,— My

love for her will nev - er die!"

now in the chap - el Lau - ra prays— For her Tom - my who

passed a - way;— It was just for Lau - ra he lived and died,— A -

lone in the chap - el she can hear him cry;—

TUTTI FRUTTI

Words and Music by R. PENNIM
and D. La BOST

THE TWIST

Words and Music by HANK BALLARD

UNDER THE BOARDWALK

Words and Music by
ARTIE RESNICK & KENNY YOUNG

WAH-WATUSI

Words and Music by KAL MANN
and DAVE APPELL

VENUS

Words and Music by
ED MARSHAL[L]

YAKETY-YAK

Words and Music by JERRY LEI
and MIKE STOL

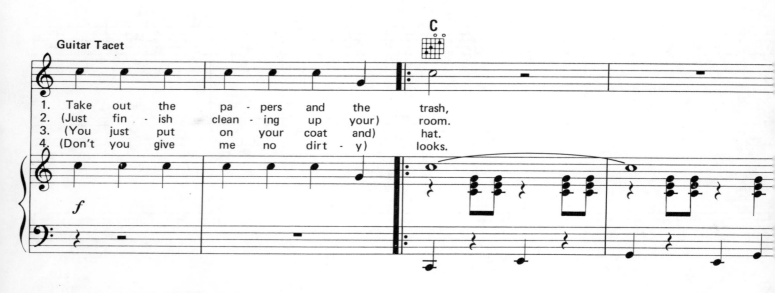

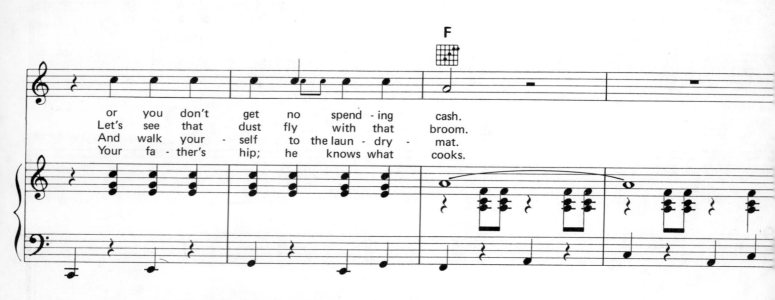

WOOLY BULLY

Moderately

Words and Music
DOMINGO SAMU

1. Mat - ty told Hat - ty
2,3. *See additional lyrics*

A - bout a thing she saw.

Had two big horns

126

Bul - ly___

Eb7

Additional Lyrics

2. Hatty told Matty
   Let's don't take no chance,
   Let's not be L 7
   Come and learn to dance
   Wooly bully — wooly bully —
   Wooly bully — wooly bully — wooly bully.

3 Matty told Hatty
   That's the thing to do,
   Get yo' someone really
   To pull the wool with you —
   Wooly bully — wooly bully
   Wooly bully — wooly bully — wooly bully.

Piano/Vocal MIXED FOLIOS

Presenting the best variety of piano/vocal folios. Music includes guitar chord frames.

"BEST EVER" SERIES

BEST BIG BAND SONGS EVER 00359129
the greatest big band songs ever, including: Ballin' The Jack • Basin Street Blues • ogie Woogie Bugle Boy • The Continental • Don't Get Around Much Anymore • In Mood • Opus One • Satin Doll • Sentimental Journey • String Of Pearls • and more.

BROADWAY SONGS EVER 00309155
70 tunes featuring: All The Things You Are • Bewitched • Don't Cry For Me Ar- na • I Could Have Danced All Night • If Ever I Would Leave You • Memory • Ol' Man • You'll Never Walk Alone • and many more.

BEST COUNTRY SONGS EVER 00359498
-time country hits including: Always On My Mind • Could I Have This Dance • God The U.S.A. • Help Me Make It Through The Night • Islands In The Stream • and more.

BEST EASY LISTENING SONGS EVER 00359193
100 beautiful songs including: Around The World • Candle On The Water • Day y • A Foggy Day • I'll Never Smile Again • Just In Time • Manhattan • Strangers e Night • and many more.

BEST SONGS EVER 00359224
-time hits including: Climb Ev'ry Mountain • Edelweiss • Feelings • Here's That Day • I Left My Heart In San Francisco • Love Is Blue • People • Stardust • Sunrise, t • Woman In Love • many more.

BEST STANDARDS EVER Volume 1 00359231
Volume 2 00359232
volume collection of 140 vintage and contemporary standards including: All hings You Are • Endless Love • The Hawaiian Wedding Song • I Left My Heart Francisco • Misty • My Way • Old Cape Cod • People • Wish You Were Here • Yes- y's Songs • and many more.

CONTEMPORARY SONGS — 50 Top Hits 00359190
of the best, most recent hits, featuring: Any Day Now • Deja Vu • Endless Love ndance . . . What A Feeling • I.O.U. • Islands In The Stream • September Morn ough The Years • You Needed Me • and many more.

KNOWN LATIN SONGS 00359194
ulous selection of over 50 favorite Latin songs including: Blame It On The Bossa • A Day In The Life Of A Fool • The Girl From Ipanema • Poinciana • Quando, o, Quando • Spanish Eyes • Watch What Happens • Yellow Days • and more!

ADWAY DELUXE 00309245
Smash Broadway songs including: Cabaret • Edelweiss • I Could Have Danced All • Memory • Send In The Clowns • Seventy Six Trombones • Sunrise, Sunset • Remember • What Kind Of Fool Am I? • A Wonderful Guy • and many more.

EMPORARY HIT DUETS 00359501
t duets from today's biggest pop stars includes Don't Go Breaking My Heart • ss Love • Ebony And Ivory • Say, Say, Say • You Don't Bring Me Flowers • and

EMPORARY LOVE SONGS 00359496
ection of today's best love songs including Endless Love • September Morn • gs • Through The Years • and more.

GOLD UPDATE 00359740
70 Hits from the 80's including: All Through The Night • Endless Love • Every n You Take • Fortress Around Your Heart • Memory • Miami Vice • One Night In ok • Sentimental Street • What's Love Got To Do With It • Total Eclipse Of The • and more!

EN ENCYCLOPEDIA OF FOLK MUSIC 00359905
t collection of more than 180 classic folk songs including songs of true love, un- ed and false love, spirituals, songs of the west, jolly reunions, international and singing the blues.

DMA MOSES SONGBOOK 00359938
tiful collection of over 80 traditional and folk songs highlighted by the fascinat- intings of Grandma Moses. Features: America The Beautiful • The Glow Worm ysuckle Rose • I'll Be Home On Christmas Day • Look To The Rainbow • Sudden- re's A Valley • Sunrise, Sunset • Try To Remember • and many, many more!

NGS FROM THE 70's & 80's 00310665
the top songs from the Billboard Hot 100 charts of the 70's and 80's, featur- very Breath You Take • How Deep Is Your Love • Joy To The World • Laughter Rain • Love Will Keep Us Together • Love's Theme • Maneater • Maniac • Morn- ain • Stayin' Alive • and more.

150 OF THE MOST BEAUTIFUL SONGS EVER
Perfect Bound - 00360735   Plastic Comb Bound - 00360734
Bali Ha'i • Bewitched • Could I Have This Dance • I Remember It Well • I'll Be Seeing You • If I Ruled The World • Love Is Blue • Memory • Songbird • When I Need You • more.

R & B BALLADS 00360870
25 wonderful ballads, including: Careless Whisper • Earth Angel • Just Once • Sara Smile • Sexual Healing • Shake You Down • and more.

ROCK REVIVAL SONGBOOK 00360940
40 top hits from the early rock era, featuring: A Teenager In Love • At The Hop • Blue- berry Hill • Chantilly Lace • Chapel Of Love • Don't Be Cruel • Duke Of Earl • Earth Angel • Great Balls Of Fire • The Twist • Wooly Bully • and more.

70 CONTEMPORARY HITS 00361056
A super collection of 70 hits featuring: Every Breath You Take • Time After Time • Memory • Wake Me Up Before You Go-Go • Endless Love • Islands In The Stream • Through The Years • Valotte • and many more.

60 CONTEMPORARY HITS 00361078
Featuring: September Morn • Somewhere Out There • Song Sung Blue • These Dreams • Time After Time • What's Love Got To Do With It • You Are My Lady • and many more!

23 AWARD WINNING POP HITS 00361385
23 of the best including Don't Cry Out Loud • Flashdance . . . What A Feeling • Memo- ry • You Needed Me • and more.

24 AWARD WINNING POP HITS 00361384
Featuring: Copacabana • Fire And Rain • Holding Back The Years • Longer • Michelle • Piano Man • Sara • Stand By Me • Somewhere Out There • We Built This City • With Or Without You • and more.

VIDEO ROCK HITS 00361457
A collection of hits from today's biggest video artists — Tiffany, George Michael, Tracy Chapman, Debbie Gibson, Sting, Billy Ocean, Michael Jackson, Patrick Swayze and others! 21 songs including: Could've Been • Fast Car • Foolish Beat • Get Outta My Dreams, Get Into My Car • Man In The Mirror • New Sensation • Tell It To My Heart • and many more.

YOUNG AT HEART SONGBOOK 00361820
101 light hearted, fun loving favorites: Alley Cat • Bandstand Boogie • Bye Bye Blues • Five Foot Two, Eyes Of Blue • I Could Have Danced All Night • Let Me Entertain You • The Sound Of Music • Tiny Bubbles • True Love • Young At Heart • and more.

THE DECADE SERIES

SONGS OF THE 1920's 00361122
Ain't Misbehavin' • April Showers • Baby Face • California Here I Come • Five Foot Two, Eyes Of Blue • I Can't Give You Anything But Love • and more

SONGS OF THE 1930's 00361123
All Of Me • The Continental • I Can't Get Started • I'm Getting Sentimental Over You • In The Mood • The Lady Is A Tramp • Love Letters In The Sand • and more.

SONGS OF THE 1940's 00361124
Come Rain Or Come Shine • God Bless The Child • How High The Moon • The Last Time I Saw Paris • Moonlight In Vermont • A String Of pearls • Swinging On A Star • Tuxedo Junction • You'll Never Walk Alone • and more.

SONGS OF THE 1950's 00361125
Blue Suede Shoes • Blue Velvet • Here's That Rainy Day • Love Me Tender • Misty • Rock Around The Clock • Satin Doll • Tammy • Three Coins In The Fountain • and more.

SONGS OF THE 1960's 00361126
By The Time I Get To Phoenix • California Dreamin' • Can't Help Falling In Love • Downtown • Happy Together • I Want To Hold Your hand • Love Is Blue • More • Strangers In The Night • and more.

PIANO ALPHABETICAL SONGFINDER 72000004
Complete listing of the thousands of songs included in the Easy Piano and Piano/ Vocal/Guitar books. Song titles are cross-referenced to the books in which they can be found. Available free of charge from your local music store. Or, write to: HAL LEONARD PUBLISHING CORP. • P.O. Box 13819, Milwaukee, WI 53213

HL HAL LEONARD PUBLISHING CORPORATION
For more information, see your local music dealer, or write to:
P.O. Box 13819 • Milwaukee, WI 53213